Roly meets the monster

WRITTEN BY EDEL WIGNELL

ILLUSTRATED BY NEIL CURTIS

"Let's vote for our favorite rabbit," said
Mr. Martin, the teacher.

He put the names on a chart: Peter Rabbit,
Benjamin Bunny, Snowy, Humbug,
George, Miffy, Shadrach, and many others.

Roly Rabbit watched from his hutch; *his*
name wasn't included. The favorite was
Peter Rabbit.

Why did Peter Rabbit get the most votes?
Roly sat and thought. Suddenly he knew:
Peter Rabbit had won because he was
adventurous.

Roly was a good pet—always obeying
the rules. He was just like Flopsy, Mopsy,
and Cottontail—and no one voted for them
either. He knew how to open his hutch, but
he came out only when he was invited.
Sometimes he was allowed to hop around
the classroom, but he had never been into

the playground. Edwina had told him about
the dogs out there, so he didn't want to go.
A door led into a corridor, but Roly had
never wanted to investigate.
Now, like Peter Rabbit, he wanted
adventure. He opened the hutch door and
hopped out.

Then Roly remembered something.
Ms. Meraka, the principal, had a monster in
the foyer. She had won a blue ribbon for
the Champion Exhibit at the Horticultural
Society Show with a *Monstera Deliciosa*.
Last week she had invited the children
to see it. They came back, amazed.
"What a monster!"
"It's enormous!"
"It's taller than my dad."
Roly paused and looked at their pictures;
he shivered at the sight of the long fingers
and the terrifying eyes.

Now Roly remembered hearing the words
edible and *delicious*.

He knew that Peter Rabbit had been
warned about an accident. His father had
been edible, and Mr. McGregor had baked
him in a pie which, no doubt, had been
delicious.

But Peter Rabbit hadn't been deterred.
Heart thumping, Roly hopped into the
corridor.

He looked right and left and saw doors
opening into classrooms. On the left, the
corridor led to the foyer.

Which way would he go?

Then he smelled something leafy; it was fresh
and enticing, so he moved towards it.

He peeped furtively around the foyer,
ready to escape. The monster wasn't there,
and Roly was glad to see a huge plant with
drooping foliage – a perfect hiding place.

Roly investigated two rooms: one was the
principal's office, and the other a
storeroom. No monster.

It was evening—the time of day when
rabbits long to scrabble and scratch in
sandy soil. Ahhhhh!

Roly was hungry, so he started a leafy
banquet. Once he had begun, he couldn't
stop: it was delicious.
He ate and ate and ate, until… after a
while… he felt rather sick and wished he
had some parsley.

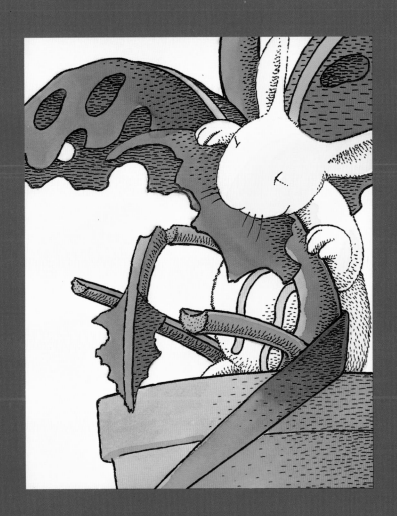

By now it was nighttime, and a light
snapped on outside.
Suddenly the monster appeared!

Roly ran! But he had lost direction.
He rushed into the principal's office. He
rushed into the storeroom. He rushed past
the monster into the corridor and went in
the wrong direction, for he had forgotten
the way back.

He sat down to rest, for he was out of
breath and trembling with fright. Soon he
returned, going lippety-lippety, not very
fast.

He sneaked past the monster again and,
at last, found his room. Thankfully he
hopped into his hutch and closed the door.

Next day there was a terrible to-do! The news spread quickly throughout the school. "Someone has attacked Ms. Meraka's *Monstera Deliciosa.*"
"Who could it be?"
And in Mr. Martin's classroom, there was even more concern:
"Roly is sick."
Everyone worried. "Poor Roly! What's wrong with him?"

Then Edwina discovered sandy soil on his paws and smelled *Monstera Deliciosa* on his breath. She told all the children.

They laughed and crowded around with admiring comments.

"Roly, you naughty rabbit!"

"You're in for it!"

"Oh, you *are* bad!"

This praise made Roly feel a little better, but he knew he would be punished. So he wasn't surprised when Mr. Martin made him stay in the hutch all day and didn't let the children give him any lettuce leaves or carrots.

From his hutch he watched the children
make a new book which they called,
Roly Meets the Monster.

They put it on the shelf beside the other
rabbit stories.

But the best part of the day was the revote
for the favorite rabbit. Everyone clapped
when Roly won.

"I've got dibs on taking Roly home next
weekend," said Edwina.

"Thank you," said Mr. Martin. "Thank you
very much indeed."

Then Edwina whispered to Roly, "My
Mom's got hundreds of potted plants, and it's
my job to water and look after them. Will
you help?